Tissue

Naomi Karmue

BookLeaf Publishing

India | USA | UK

Presentation by *BookLeaf Publishing*

Web: www.bookleafpub.com

E-mail: info@bookleafpub.com

ISBN: 9789358313147

First edition 2023

To Abigail. If you ever want to understand your godmother more. Here are my thoughts, and my tissue. Dedicated to you.

ACKNOWLEDGEMENT

I want to thank God, first of all. If not for him I wouldn't have the ability to write this collection. My father and mother have been, and will always be, my greatest supporters. My father, for reading and critiquing all of my work. My mother, for giving me the chance and pushing me to take it. My friend, Ashley, has read most, if not all, of these poems. Reminding me that my mind is not a total haze. Lastly, my inspiration. I'll say no names or titles.

Present Dictionary

Whispers win through the cranial beat.
They do not null the pounding,
there goes the band, perpetually marching along.
Content; live within it.
Embrace; define it with new meaning.
It is deemed becoming.
It adapts. Evolves.

Spoken word stains like the slip of a scar.
The seal skin feels heavy now. It goes slipping
from my fingers.
Adapt; find the strength.
Evolve; perfect the clay.
It is not enough.

Screams run the paths like fire.
Empty crevices are filled.
Ownership is marked by the scorched.
Consumption; bite, chew, swallow.
Digest; to rid of excess.

Then, the all-while hush.
Until it is back once more
insistent in its urge:
content, embrace

adapt, evolve
consume, digest
For numbness in the noise.

Damned to Hell

This grave is a cabin of desolation.
I made my peace.
In the depths of despair,
here I was left.
Deposited in my anguish.
They stored me beneath the dirt
so I made home in the darkness.
Then Lord Anubis walked.
Shattered the visage.

I believed in the docile dog.
He leads the living to his master
for it is his command.
Beguiling is he who christens himself Death.
For it is he who led to life eternal.

In this way,
the scales were tipped.
Justification was sought and none was found.
The feather stood above me.
So came the dog, once again
to drag me to true death.
Damnation eternal.

Pretenses

Deep breaths baby.
I'm going to kill myself.

There's beauty in my madness.
I need no methods.

You don't need to understand
You are not invited.

In this, I am sticking true.
I only want to see the end in your hands,

Be not swift to catch me.
Let the rope around my neck tighten.

Allow my spine to snap.
For I have grown tired of this incessant march.

Where is the end?
Do you remember the beginning?

My life is in my hands.
One simple sense of control.

Don't meet me on my deathbed.

Promise you'll let me go cold.

Your love was sweet.
I'll savor it.

You remember it when I pass on.

Decomposure

Paint me black---
I was born covered in brown
Eventually, clothed in white---
I'll stand by idle.

A marionette to the people
I have become the susceptible canvas.

Keep me bleak---
I'd prefer---
I'm made beautiful through hues
of color and light.

This; it is hung from the wall.
Gawked, squawked at.

I preen my best---
I am something to look at---
sit exactly as posed.
Though the light is not mine.

When it is at its brightest
that is when they appear.

The shadows---

run the paint---
cut the strings---
paint me black.

Snap, Crackle

The mass around your head is enormous
Doesn't mean that everyone can see it, though
You sit, crunched up,
Your face, scrunched up.
Your lips are steel enforced.
Nothing comes out, yet everything flows at
once.
You bare your teeth
They're sharpened, poised to bite at anything
that comes within distance
How you play now
just with thunder and lightning,
Striking and booming up a storm.
I don't like that.
I'm waiting too
I'm most positive
Your negative energy's gonna be aimed at me
one day
And when it is,
my aim will be true.

Number 99.0999

Status, state percentage
Goal: optimal stasis
Number: ten

Flowers wither and die
I have run through them
Their death, unnatural
in vain
I destroy beauty
Can I bear, oh my own hands

Status, state percentage
Goal: optimal stasis
Number: twenty-five

My mother sings
Sometimes it's horrid
Often, it's light
That's how he finds her
songs tranquiling the night
She's beauty at that age
They're wonders of nigh
The song they sing is a symphony
though, no longer something
I dearly need

Status, state percentage
Goal: optimal stasis
Number: fifty-three

It's daunting, the pressure
crows watch my feet
They know,
I'm chasing a natural life
constrained by an unnatural energy
I run but I can't run
I hide by I can't hide
I want...well,
I'm still looking

Status, state percentage
Goal: optimal stasis
Number: seventy-

Queen of the Earth
Lord of the Stars
I'm second, third, fourth, fifth
to many things
Though, my crown is big enough
Optimal Status

Of Worlds (pt. 2)

Enemies of my progress
stand behind me.

Eyes see your mouths moving
with curses to my name
Yet, ears hear only the words from mine

You disagree,
to disagree
be that you are only against me

I lose myself in your labyrinths.
Your hatred the dim torch guiding me
to the transient exit.
You tell me, that I can't turn back.
No, I can't go the way that I came.

Undo the done
I move forward
inch away from that knife.
Quickly I go
and you call to me
I turn to look
and you've put obstructions in my path

Slowly I move
and I am trampled.
You are the predator stalking my home.
I've left the door open.

The sheet of paper is torn
don't crumple it
it's already thin.
Still, you mercilessly submerge it.
Surprisingly, you are shocked
watching as it disintegrates.

Death to the destroyer.
You don't see the hidden written.
You don't want to know
my true promise
nor my pride.

Stand behind me.
I'll keep my stride.

False Gods

These are the idols
that stand on my chest
caress my lungs
then compress them

These are the pretenses
Of goodness and of peace
that kiss and bite
my lips and my cheeks

These are the charlatans
with masks, the false faces
scatter their praise, their lies
in all of my places

These are my friends,
acquaintances, surrounds
Happiness for them,
they don't cease pulling me down.

To Him

Mommy says to pray
I know that God hears
so I break my knees
and my heart I bear

I bow my head
before I lay to rest
and I sing his praise
thank him for strength
thank him for his tests

Give me relief,
I beg. A pause in this life
Sturdify my belief
protect me from strife.

If your will is true-
No, Lord, I mean mine
Let both our wills align

Inquired of Existence

What constitutes the shades between black and
white?
The difference:
she punched,
he stabbed
a question of morality?
Is there fickle balance between mortality?
The edge is sharp on one side
it's dull and brittle on the other
though the blade remains a blade.
What opens arms to welcome
but turn up noses in dismal?

The Black Substance

There's a force behind his walk
A tempered cocky breeze
It's hidden with charisma
His mind worn on his sleeve

He floats his way merrily
Through buildings of education prestige
A golden egg amongst golden eggs
they tell him
They expect his life of ease

Things shatter sometime. Around him
the ground he walks now glass
He doesn't understand this world
He isn't stable enough to pass

But he stumbles his way through it
Crawls on his knees 'cause he can't
Reaches toward a limelight
Coping, straying from the mend

In this other land
In this forefront of time
His auger dies
As he stumbles on the devastating chime.

Within his hand
The perfect drug
Befouling the man he could've been
Once was.

Life Matters

Busting heads,
Brain matter oozes,
>Onto the concrete road
What sits between
>What has been
>And will be

Tearing throats
>Who's that piece of tongue for?
Where's their song
>Amid the hush,
rush, bust of
Wanna sees and
>Born to hope

Empty eyes
Cause they're not here
No reason to be
>When what they've
>Wanted to see and
>Hoped for has been done

Except When It Doesn't

He got shot for that
That life, poofed
He survived though

He got caught with that
The vultures, of course, had
just been waiting
circling overhead

There're no poofs or
quick deaths now
He's chewed, pummeled
Left for dead

The old man
arrives slowly
His cane
senseless impalement

Love's Lover (pt.2)

Love's Lover is insane.
What good is gratitude?

There's a pit.
It's deep. The fall down is long.
Does it ever end?
There is honestly no way
no way
to tell unless I fall in.
It's not worth the crack,
crackle, bones to bits and ashes.

I'm insane, I know.
Crazy beyond understanding.
Swayed by love's lover.
And still,
what good is gratitude?

I mean it.
Words fall from my lips.
Hello, fly, taste honey.
My honey is so bitter.
My tongue, cracked and dry.

Is there more for me to want?

More than.
More than.
More than.
I want-

to know
What good is gratitude?

Does it feel good this way?
My bets, my bets, my bet
is...
No.

Shine better, please.
Ignite me.
Else, damn you all.

Politely Please

Twist me up in your velvet rope.
The caress is soft against my wrists.
I stretch when you pull.
Only adjust myself to more comfortably fit.
You tell me, "just a little more"
And I move along to your whim
Lying still in your company,
just because you want me to.
Pangs in my abdomen.
A desert in my throat.
It gets bad.
I let it, for you.
But it gets too much.
Too soon, I need.
Not a storm, not even a drizzle.
A small drop.
Enough to satiate me.
And I hope, silently.
Maybe you'll do this.
For me.
I don't mean the push-pull
(though I am always pushing)
Once
Satiate me,
I plead.

But nothing.
You stare blankly at my audacity.
I'm left
Sorry.

Stilettos

Fat old man,
hold the p-h-.
Clean yourself up.
Lying there, bile staining your skin.

When are you going to pull yourself together?
That off-color muscle tee.
Those glazed, never-tracking eyes.
Just a bit of cash, you say

Which ditch will I dig you out of?
How many cells have you seen?
Find inhibition.
Find courage.

Bring back those days of concrete
and chalk.
Milky ice
and sharing pots.

Self medication is out of date.
brickle and weathered now.
It's not the same when it rings in your ears.
Out of you, into me.

Crazy old fool.
You steal my thoughts.
Step on my chest with your place in my heart.
On my mind.

Of Friends and Arrangements

You,
are a dandy little fish.
With all those shiny scales.
That puffed up chest.
Those silver eyes.

Aren't you a mouthwatering sight.
I already taste
that soft white meat
melting on my tongue

You bite my line.
I pull you up.
You smile.
Up to something.

Sizzle, pop, squelch
The delicious sounds you make
in the hot pot.
Warm fish, butter, a bit of salt.

I sit to eat.
The knife, the fork
The side of lemon.
I inhale your sweet, sweet scent.

You're soft,
On my lips, in my mouth
Like I thought
But the taste

Sour, foul
I see that smile
Staring up at me.
That same, silver eye

I see.
You knew.
You, vile little fish

Purple Rain

I call it love my newest creation blank face it's
presented to a crowd
its laughed at called names they ridicule it and
for shame for shame
for shame for shame not that kind not like that
what do we get what
do you get what about what i want what about
my label what about
what about what about shut up i say this love is
good love love that
makes sense they call me foolish stand up leave
and the kids they
cry and the wives sob and the men weep and the
one in between
rejoice because they don't have that love but
inside feel the same
even worse without it my work is scrapped i
shred papers start
fires with burning infernos that spread into my
heart into the hearts
the world turns gray black deep ugly purple in
my eyes the film
gloss it over evil i seethe ignorant stupid evil all
of you then i realize
it's me

Gentleman Luck

Luck be no lady
He's a cold-blooded white man
He forces his way into the lives of many
He takes his piece
leaves behind only contraband.
He arrives with proclamations of superiorities.
He knows better
won't let the peaceful dying lie and be.
He stirs up trouble
He fixes lives,
and he walks away.
Not taking his pain
leaving behind his strife,
They call for his help
relish briefly by his side.
Then he's gone
just as fast
nothing left but split ends.

Rose Colored

Is my face one of kindness
Bat my eyes, flutter my lashes
I'm not trying to draw you in

Still, you come
Your doll reminisce
already made up to look
like who you think I am

You make my lips pink
Narrow my waist
soften the bite of my voice

I slap off those glasses
And suddenly you see
my face is crevices and dry peaks
kindness doesn't become me

10.28.23

Who's dead
Like cockroaches the news swarms
Like bedbugs, it spreads
Like the worm, it rings
over and over in the drums
of everyone

Who's dead
People look at each other
searching for signs of decay
They sniff, like bloodhounds
as though they can taste the rotting flesh

Who's dead
It's an influenza
The people quarantine
death spreads
who's got the death touch

Who's dead
The hologlyph appears
Suddenly, starkly overhead
Glitchy until it's not

Just there

Written in white bold:

YOU'RE DEAD
the hitch in her breath
oceans form to her island
She's dead.
Already, she feels the cold touch